MW00745214

Peace . . .
in Spite of
Panic

by Charles R. Swindoll

Zondervan Publishing House
Grand Rapids, Michigan

A Division of HarperCollins*Publishers*

Peace . . . In Spite of Panic: Finding Calm in a Chaotic World
© 1984, 1995 by Charles R. Swindoll.

Requests for information should be addressed to:
Zondervan Publishing House
5300 Patterson Avenue S.E.
Grand Rapids, Michigan 49530

ISBN 0-310-20087-3

Unless otherwise identified, all Scripture references are from the New American Standard Bible, © The Lockman Foundation 1960, 1962, 1963, 1968, 1971, 1972, 1973, 1975, 1977. Used by permission.

Printed in the United States of America

Cover Design by DesignTeam, Brian L. Fowler

95 96 97 98 00 / ❖ DP / 5 4 3 2

Introduction

Honestly now, which virtue brings you the most satisfaction, the greatest relief, the deepest sense of comfort and reassurance? It is *peace*, isn't it? It is that tranquility of soul that frees you from fear and takes the sharp edges off your anxiety.

Peace is not only an international pursuit. It means more than an absence of warfare between opposing forces. Peace—the kind of peace I write about in this booklet—is inward peace, personal peace, a strong, rock-like confidence that things are not running wild. The Hebrew term is *shalom*, and it is frequently mentioned in the Old Testament. It has been loosely defined as the deliberate adjustment of one's life to the will of God. Or, as one of the ancient prophets put it, it's trust in action.

> The steadfast of mind Thou wilt keep in perfect peace, because he trusts in Thee. Trust in the Lord forever, for in God the Lord, we have an everlasting Rock (Isa. 26:3–4).

Indeed we do! And it has been my observation that apart from the Rock, peace is merely a distant dream ... a political football to be kicked back and forth by eloquent ambassadors . . . a philosophical fantasy . . . that glorious moment in history when everybody stands around *reloading!*

And so, let me assure you before you turn another page, the peace of which I write is inseparably connected to the only One who can provide the inner calm in which peace can survive. He is the God of heaven and earth, the Giver of eternal life through faith in His Son, Jesus Christ . . . the Source of forgiveness, the Provider of grace.

As you are about to read, in spite of panic bursting like bombshells all around us, the peace that God can give is there for us to claim like a shelter in a storm, like an anchor of hope when all seems hopeless. Like . . . well, like a rock, solid, sound, and eternally secure.

Charles R. Swindoll

Peace . . .
in Spite of
Panic

I invite you to focus your full attention on one of the rarest of all virtues. It is a virtue that everybody pursues, but very few possess on a regular basis. I'm referring to the often-longed-for but seldom-found virtue of peace.

Peace—something that is needed between nations just as badly as it is needed between neighbors. I was surprised to read one authority who said that in a total of 3,530 years of recorded civilization only 286 of those years have been spent without war taking place on this globe. And during that same period of time eight thousand peace treaties were broken.[1] We are a warring people. We are fighters deep down underneath our placid plastic cover, in spite of the fact that the cornerstone of the United Nations building reads, "They shall beat their swords into plowshares and their spears into pruning hooks; nation shall not lift up sword against nation, neither shall they learn war any more." And even though the statement of the United Nations creed reads, "Our purpose is to maintain international peace and security and to that end take effective, collective measures for the prevention and removal of threats to the peace." If the failure to bring peace to all nations wasn't so tragic, the whole idea would be hilarious.

What's true on a global level is, of course, true of individuals. Most people don't live at peace with themselves. And so it stands to reason we don't live peacefully with other people. We are basically critical and intolerant. We are in an endless wrestling match with insecurity, a lack of confidence, a struggle with a purpose and place in life, and the pursuit of freedom from worry and anxiety. That's true among Christians as well as non-Christians. How very, very few live a life that is calm, deliberate, free from anxiety.

Well, you say, "That's fine if you're passive by nature, but if you're a leader, then you simply have to worry a lot. Especially strong natural leaders! You certainly have to be involved in the whole tiring process of getting people motivated. And that certainly leads to anxiety."

No. As a matter of fact, it shouldn't.

Frank Goble, in his book *Excellence in Leadership,* includes a particular chart that is of interest to me. It's a chart on psychological maturity among leaders on one side, and then on the other side he lists the immature characteristics. Among the thirty-four characteristics that are contrasted, four read as follows: "The immature leader is critical, emotional, tense, and impulsive. The mature leader is tolerant, calm, relaxed, and patient." Even an authority in the field of leadership admits that it takes peace to be a good leader.

PEACE ACCORDING TO A PROPHET NAMED ISAIAH

Tucked away in the twenty-sixth chapter of Isaiah are two verses we need to blow the dust off of every once in a while. And I'd like to do that right now, even before we observe and examine an exemplary model—the apostle Paul, a strong natural leader who lived at peace with himself and with others. I want us to see from the prophet Isaiah (who lived eight hundred years before Paul's day) some basic principles about peace itself.

I'd like you to take note not only of what these verses are saying, but also of what they mean to you personally. I want to draw my remarks from the colorful Hebrew language, which is the original text of Isaiah 26:3–4. Remember, the prophet is not writing about international peace. He's talking about an individual at peace with himself, with God, and with others.

> The steadfast of mind Thou wilt keep in perfect peace, because he trusts in Thee. Trust in the Lord forever, for in God the Lord, we have an everlasting Rock (Isa. 26:3–4).

Steadfast is from a term that means "to lean, to rest, to support." It's the idea of being sustained as a result of leaning on something that is supporting you. The words *of mind* come from one verb that means "to frame," or "to fashion, to form." And in the original Hebrew language this particular construction has the idea of "a frame of mind."

If you put the two thoughts together, they convey this: "A frame of mind that is receiving support from leaning and therefore is being sustained." And that brings us to the main verb, *Thou wilt keep.* The term means "to guard from danger, *to watch over.*" And it is so rendered in Isaiah 42:6.

The frame of mind that is being supported as a result of leaning, Thou, Lord, will watch over with "shalom, shalom." Not literally "perfect peace," but "peace, peace." In the original Hebrew language a term was repeated for emphasis. So here the idea is of an unending security, a sense of uninterrupted, perpetual rest and calmness. It doesn't come from some human being. According to the prophet's words, it comes from the God upon whom the person leans.

Now, how does God know when to give us that rest? Well, it says in verse 3, *because we trust in Him.* In Arabic (occasionally closely related to the Hebrew), the term for *trust* has a very picturesque meaning: "to throw one's self down upon his face."

I think of a trampoline when I think of that imagery. I think of jumping up and down and letting all of my weight fall in an almost relaxed manner on a trampoline. You can just feel yourself bouncing off that stretched-out piece of thick vinyl.

Now, the thought is that you abandon yourself to all the other crutches that you can lean on, and you place all of your anxiety, all of your being, your circumstance, on the only One who can support you.

Can He support? Good question. Read on . . . it says that He is *an everlasting rock.* Now it would hurt us to fall on a large, solid rock. But it's not the idea of falling you must remember. It is the idea of *leaning.* It's the thought of leaning on something that will be perpetually supportive, solid enough to sustain your weight.

Now if you put all of it together, the paraphrase would read like this: "A frame of mind that is receiving support from leaning and, therefore, is being sustained, Thou,

Lord, will watch over with infinite calm.
Because he leans fully and relies upon You
and none other, You, Lord God, are the everlasting support." This is the scene of a tran-
quil, restful mind in spite of circumstances.
What a marvelous, limitless promise!

I recently came across Isaiah 16:3 and
am glad I did! It has been a sustaining force
and source of strength in my own life, for
that was literally "the week that was." You
may have heard me say that before, but that
was it, believe me. There won't be another
like it. Hear that, Lord? Maybe I should pray,
"Let there be no other!" I mean, there were
disappointments. There were jolts. There
were surprises. There were areas of sickness
we had to deal with in our family. There
were the constant demands. But behind the
scenes, I want to tell you, there was a great
measure of peace. There were times when I
became anxious. Three or four times I was
really anxious, but for the most part when I
claimed the truth and entered into a personal experience of verses 3 and 4, there was
a distinct difference. When I said, "Lord, I
consciously now lean on You and I abandon
all of my strength for this situation," He held
me up.

I suppose the reason I lay that on you
right now is because I want you to know this
is not print from a page in the Bible. This is
biblical theory that works in the trenches of
life. It begs to be applied. It reaches out of

the page with long arms and stretching hands saying. "Take me. I'm yours, Christian, please take hold of me. You have to claim me." That's what I want you to do as a result of reading these things from Paul's experience in Acts 19.

PEACE ACCORDING TO
A PASTOR NAMED PAUL.

Let's turn to the New Testament (eight hundred years later in time, but still nineteen-hundred-plus years back from our perspective) and let's look at Acts 19:21–41. In these twenty-one verses it is not difficult to pick out three very significant moments that normally bring anxiety, but they didn't in Paul's experience.

To begin with, Paul is shutting down a very successful ministry. I say "shutting down," but perhaps I should say he is leaving it in order to go on his way to new vistas of ministry. Now, Ephesus has been his "headquarters" for a three-year period of ministry. Verse 21 looks back: "Now after these things were finished . . ."

When you read that in your Bible, remember there's an invisible arrow that points back up to verses 1–20. And remember, you have to integrate verses of Scripture with their historical context, much like a setting of a precious gem is placed in a ring. Every precious verse of Scripture fits into its own unique setting. Now the setting of verse

21 is what we could call a successful ministry, but not one without problems or diffi-
culties.

> After these things were finished [he now
> looks to the future], Paul purposed in the
> spirit to go to Jerusalem after he had
> passed through Macedonia and Achaia,
> saying, "After I have been there, I must
> also see Rome."

An obvious characteristic of good leadership is goals and objectives. There are
dreams. There are plans. There are goals in
mind. An individual who lives just from day
to day is really not having a purposeful life.
But Paul is not like this. He has a goal, and it
is clear. He hopes ultimately to reach Rome.
Why Rome? Why is that so significant? Well,
Rome was the Oval Office of the world. It
was the place of ultimate clout. The emperor
lived there. Saints lived in Caesar's Palace.
Paul knew that if he could reach Rome, he
could reach some of the most influential
Christians of the known world. And also,
quite probably, he could gain an audience
with the emperor himself. He longed to
speak to Caesar about Jesus Christ.

PEACE AMIDST
UNFULFILLED DREAMS

There are some of you who read these
words today who have dreams and goals.
Some of you have never shared your deepest
dreams and your highest goals, but they are

there nevertheless. And the tendency is to be frustrated before you reach the ultimate goals and dreams of your life.

I want to show you something about Paul. He was at peace with those dreams. See verse 22. Remember the dream now, "I must see Rome."

> And having sent into Macedonia two of those who ministered to him, Timothy and Erastus, he himself stayed in Asia for a while.

If you check several verses of Scripture, you will discover that Paul was in Ephesus three years in all. Chapter 20, verse 31 tells us that. Chapter 19, verse 8 says he began with a three-month ministry in the synagogue. Chapter 19, verse 10 says he later ministered for two years at the school of Tyrannus, so we've got twenty-seven months accounted for. But he was in Ephesus thirty-six months. Meaning what? Meaning that nine of the thirty-six months were spent (verse 22) staying in Asia after he got the dream to go to Rome.

When you have a dream and a purpose and some goals in life that you really want to see occur, your tendency is to leave immediately and to get on with the goals rather than to stay faithful in the assignments of the present.

Allow me to give you the first of three definitions of peace. Here it is: *peace is the ability to remain faithful in spite of the panic of unrealized or unfulfilled dreams.* If you forget that, you'll be frustrated and your peace will quickly disappear.

When I entrust my frame of mind to Him and I lean on my everlasting Rock, He supports me with the ability to stay at the task as I let Him open the doors of the dream.

Now, some of you need that more than others. (I personally need it a great deal.) When you do lean on Him, you may anticipate that things will level out, and at least as you remain faithful in doing things that are less than exciting, your life will become calm and easy to handle. Right? Wrong. As a matter of fact, it's like the old saying: "Cheer up. Things could be worse. So I cheered up and sure enough, they got worse!" Paul may have thought, "Well, things are gonna get better. I know that these last few months will just run along rather smoothly and unruffled." But they didn't. Things just got worse.

Look at the next verse. Now this is after Paul has been willing to stay at the task with Rome on his heart (verse 23). *"About that time . . ."* That's the way it happens. Just about the time you get out of your prayer closet and you've got it all worked out, everything breaks loose. Look at the rest of verse 23:

There arose no small disturbance concerning the Way [which was a first-century label for Christianity].

About the time you get things settled in your heart and promise, "Lord, I'm not gonna panic; I'm gonna leave those dreams with You," no small disturbance occurs.

PEACE AMIDST UNPLEASANT CIRCUMSTANCES

Well, what was the problem? Verse 24 and following describes it. First, Paul is publicly accused by a man who doesn't even know him.

> For a certain man named Demetrius, a silversmith, who made silver shrines of Artemis, was bringing no little business to the craftsmen; these he gathered together with the workmen of similar trades, and said, "Men, you know that our prosperity depends upon this business."

Now what's going on? Well, I take it that this was sort of like a century-one trade union. It was a guild of men who worked in the same trade. They worked with silver and they built little silver shrines of the temple of Artemis, also called Diana.

The temple of Artemis was the major shrine erected and housed in the city of Ephesus. The Ephesians believed that it fell from Jupiter, from the heavens, and landed in that particular location known at that time as the

city of Ephesus. And there they built their
city around this shrine.

In a way similar to the Muslim pilgrim-
age to Mecca, many travelers would journey
to Ephesus to worship at the shrine of
Artemis. This prompted the silversmiths to
build the trinkets—the little souvenirs—for
tourists to buy. Maybe they hung them
around their necks or put 'em on their cloth-
ing or stuck 'em on their chariots. Whatever
they did with 'em, the craftsmen made a
bundle off the tourists from those tiny silver
trinkets.

One day a craftsman named Demetrius
realized that their business was taking a turn
for the worse. Why? He tells us in verse 26:

> You see and hear that not only in
> Ephesus, but in almost all of Asia, this
> Paul has persuaded and turned away a
> considerable number of people, saying
> that gods made with hands are not gods
> at all.

You can just hear Paul say that in the
school of Tyrannus, can't you?

You see, when you have bought into this
lifestyle all of your life, then you have a blind
spot, even though you are growing in Christ.
This was true of some of these new Ephesian
Christians who had forever been worship-
ping at the shrine of Artemis. But Paul
explained to them, "You don't worship there

anymore. You worship the one deity, the Lord God of heaven, Jesus Christ Himself."

And so they gave up their trinkets and spread the word as they were won to Christ. And now, perhaps by the thousands, people were leaving the worship of Artemis. So when they arrived on the scene at Ephesus, they no longer cared about trinkets. They stopped buying the souvenirs.

You see, the closer you get to the authentic, the less you care about the artificial. You know what's the truth so you don't need little replicas of what is false (to say nothing of what is true). You live in the realm of the abstract in your mind, and you commit yourself to the living Lord who is not seen, who is not heard (audibly). So who needs a little god or goddess? When you're serving the God of heaven, who could care less about gods on earth?

So now the craftsmen are misunderstanding Paul. They're saying, in effect, "He's to blame." Weird, isn't it? When you declare the truth you're often blamed for it even though you didn't write it. You're just declaring it. But people have no other source to turn to. They can't take a swing at God. So those who represent the Lord and His truth become the scapegoat ... the verbal punching bag. This is the place that Paul found himself in. He didn't make anybody do anything. God changed lives. But he was the voice box.

Well, look at what happened. Now remember, this is the man who has said, "Lord, I give You my future. I'm relying on You to take care of it." Things got worse. Look at the unpleasant circumstances.

Verse 27:

And not only is there danger that this trade of ours fall into disrepute, but also that the temple of the great goddess Artemis be regarded as worthless....

Verse 28:

And when they heard this and were filled with rage, they began crying out, saying, "Great is Artemis of the Ephesians!"

So they're chanting this great cry like you would chant a cheer at a ball game. "GREAT IS ARTEMIS OF THE EPHESIANS!" And they are there screaming that by the thousands. I say that because of the next verse:

And the city was filled with the confusion, and they rushed with one accord into the theater....

That theater is still standing in Ephesus, by the way. It can seat up to fifty-five thousand people. Let's say that it was nearly full—fifty thousand people or more chanting, "Great is Artemis of the Ephesians!"

And I'm sure that in the city of Ephesus Paul could hear it.

Eventually the word gets to him, "Your name is being used over there and are they mad!" In fact, verse 29 says they dragged a couple of his companions into this place that was normally the fighting arena for gladiators. Gaius and Aristarchus, Paul's traveling companions, were forced to face this mob that was now intensely angry—a very uncontrollable scene of panic.

Well, what would you do? Frankly, I'd probably take the night train to Memphis! I'd get out of there, like fast. Not Paul. Paul's at peace. Look at the next verse. A paraphrase of verse 30 would be, "Let me at 'em."

> And when Paul wanted to go into the assembly [there it is], the disciples would not let him. And also some of the Asiarchs who were friends of his sent to him and repeatedly urged him not to venture into the theater.

"Don't go out there, Paul! Man, that's maddening out there. That's . . . crazy." Yet Paul is ready to walk on the scene.

Why? First of all, he's courageous because he doesn't want Gaius and Aristarchus taking what he deserves. And second, he has peace, which causes a person to experience a degree of invincibility. When you live free of anxiety, there is this "envelope of invincibility" in your spirit. It surrounds you and you do not sense the intimidation of a mob or the fear of peril. It is nothing short of magnificent.

This brings us to the second definition: *peace is the ability to stay calm in spite of the panic of unpleasant circumstances.*

Now, in case you choose to live like this and to lean in that manner on the living Lord, I want to warn you ahead of time, *people will not understand.* If you're in a situation that calls for panic, yet you don't panic, they're going to want to know what's wrong with you. Isn't that interesting? Our mindset is so panic-oriented that when a person isn't panicked, you have to explain what's *wrong* with you. Amazing!

Are you facing an uncontrollable situation, an uncertainty? Something that you just cannot bring happiness out of? A situation that is unpleasant, uncomfortable, and dissatisfying? The Lord wants us to glorify Him and to walk in peace with Him, even though our surroundings are unpleasant.

Remember years ago when they made that first moon launch—the Apollo journey? They had these guys monitored so closely that at the time of lift-off it was reported that their pulse rate was the same as just before or just after. Can you imagine? Man, if I'd been in one of those helmets I'd have said, "We're leaving! We're going! We're on our way! Look, guys, lean over here. Look at this side." And my heart rate would've soared! Not them! They probably said, "Well, it is now 10:15. Ho hum . . . we just left. Wake up, Frank. Frank! Ralph, wake up Frank over there. He's not taking the sights in . . . (snoring sound)."

Hey, that's the result of great training. Those guys are trained. Spiritually, we can be like those astronauts. That's the whole purpose of having a permanent Rock beneath us. Otherwise, what do we have that the world doesn't have? Anyone can be at peace when everything's pleasant. That's no test. It's when "all hell breaks loose" and we don't have it together and we can't control the situation that the test comes and God is there to say, "You just lean on Me. You don't have the answer? Great! That's right where I wanted you. You can't control it? You can't manipulate it? Marvelous! Just wait! Just relax. You're not happy? You're not singing the hymns? Oh! I can give you hymns to sing that you'd never believe, and yet I don't even need to change your circumstances."

David often begins his psalms at the bottom of the valley and by the time the song is over he's at the top of the mountain. The amazing thing is that it only took him maybe a day or two to write the psalm. What changed? DAVID CHANGED. His circumstances didn't. And he's singing the hymn at the end of the song even though his circumstances are still the same.

Now Paul isn't panicked. He says, "Look. It's not fair for Gaius and Aristarchus to be out there in the theater. I need to be out there." "No. Don't go out there, Paul! Those people mean what they say." So he's wisely counseled to stay back, but the point is, he's at peace. Perpetual peace. Shalom, shalom.

If you live intimidated by people, then you need to come to terms with your lack of peace. God is bigger than any person. Learn to focus on people through the lens of God's eye and you'll never see anyone even near His match. No mob is out of His control. You can handle it. As a child of God, greater is He who is in you, than all of those people who are in the world.

You don't need to dread tomorrow. You don't need to dread your uncontrollable circumstances. It's a decision that's called "a frame of mind," otherwise known as leaning on the everlasting Rock.

Now there's one more scene where peace stands amidst panic. We have seen Paul through uncontrollable circumstances. We've also seen him with an unrealized dream. Now we find him facing an uncertain future.

PEACE AMIDST AN
UNCERTAIN FUTURE

Things actually got worse.

So then, some were shouting one thing and some another, for the assembly was in confusion, and the majority did not know for what cause they had come together (v. 32).

Can you believe that? "Why are we here?" "I don't know. Just keep shouting." "But what's the purpose?" "Keep yellin'. Keep yelling!" The mob is out there, but they don't even know why they're there.

So a guy named Alexander stands up and tries to quiet them down. He makes a defense. And verse 34 tells us this was an anti-Semitic group:

But when they recognized that he was a Jew … they shouted for about two hours, "Great is Artemis of the Ephesians!"

Now a football game lasts about three hours with commercials and halftimes, but if you count only the playing time in between downs, it's about two hours in all. Can you imagine hearing the same chant for the entire playing time of one football game? "Great is Artemis of the Ephesians!" It would drive us mad! And there are fifty thousand or more shouting that same phrase.

Guess who would hear that? Paul! You see, it didn't quiet them down. And it's uncertain what they're gonna do. They're obviously praising their goddess. Not even they know what they're going to do. They're in confusion. So there's increased pressure ... but observe how God calms them down through an unnamed clerk, a town clerk (verse 35). A clerk! Can you believe it? An otherwise insignificant no-name!

> And after quieting the multitude, the town clerk said, "Men of Ephesus, what man is there after all who does not know that the city of the Ephesians is guardian of the temple of the great Artemis, and of the image which fell down from heaven? Since then these are undeniable facts [sounds like a clerk, doesn't it?], you ought to keep calm and to do nothing rash."

Now I want you to envision this scene. Here's Paul doing that which is right, and here's a group of folks who misunderstand and believe he's doing the wrong thing. And they're at confused odds with each other. Then out of the blue, a clerk who is responsible for law and order and keeping people on the right track stands to his feet.

He gets his payroll from Rome, by the way, and he knows that Rome hates riots. He also realizes this city would soon lose its freedom if order didn't return. And nobody save Athens enjoyed their freedom more than

Ephesus. So he knows that he has to calm them down to keep himself on the payroll.

Now the beautiful part is that he doesn't know Paul and Paul doesn't know him, yet God uses *him* to quiet the multitude. Let's just follow along as he speaks.

> For you have brought these men here who are neither robbers of temples nor blasphemers of our goddess (v. 37).

That's true!

> So then, if Demetrius and the craftsmen who are with him have a complaint against any man [let's do it right], the courts are in session and proconsuls are available; let them bring charges against one another. But if you want anything beyond this, it shall be settled in the lawful assembly. (vv. 38–39).

The reason? Verse 40—Rome is watching!

> For indeed we are in danger of being accused of a riot in connection with today's affair, since there is no real cause for it; and in this connection we shall be unable to account for this disorderly gathering.

"Go home!" Verse 41:

> And after saying this he dismissed the assembly.

Who did it? A clerk.

While you and I are panicked, not

knowing about our tomorrow, God is moving clerks like pawns. We don't know the chessboard. We don't know the right moves, because we're not God. All we know is our square, if that! And we cannot move. "It's tough being a rook held in place by a bishop, ya know." We're afraid we'll get picked off. But there is peace as long as God has some pawns.

He never runs out of pawns. He never runs out of clerks. He doesn't need you to pull it off. He's doing it. When will we ever learn that? And when will we learn that God *cannot* lose?

I was so uncertain about my future as an adolescent. As some of you know, I stuttered very badly. I did not think I would ever be able to give the time of day, much less deliver a speech. And a "town clerk," my high school drama teacher, saw something in me that I didn't see. He helped me through speech therapy. I didn't know how to speak in public. But through him, I learned how. Eventually the uncertainty of my future was turned around. That was an open door that I had never even considered as a possibility. High school teachers, pay attention! You can be a "clerk" on God's board.

How about mothers who have kiddos that are struggling with who they are and where they're going and what they're doing and why they're important? Moms, in those day-to-day, constant assignments you suddenly become God's "town clerk." As such, you take charge of and free your children so that they begin to grow in confidence and can get on their way in life. It happens through the painful, consistent, daily, constant effort of motherhood. Small wonder it's under attack today!

You who hold any position at work, you who work with anyone (and that's everybody, that's all of us), the Lord wants to use us as the "clerk" in somebody else's need for peace. He simply wants us to be available.

Here's the third definition: *peace is the ability to wait patiently in spite of panic brought on by uncertainty.* Portrayed here is the panic of getting you from here to there on time. Relax! God knows just the vehicle and He's got the time table put together so that you can watch Him work.

An illustration of this would be the birth of Jesus Christ. Something we observe every year, the most significant of our holidays, is Christmas. You know the story. When Mary was pregnant and right up toward the end of her pregnancy, she was a resident permanently fixed in Nazareth (several days' journey north of Bethlehem). But the scriptures said, "It's going to happen in Bethlehem." How do you get Mary to Bethlehem so the baby can be born exactly as

God said it? Well, you must move the pawn: Caesar Augustus. Everybody in that day thought, "Ah, how great it is, or how bad it is that Caesar does this." Do you know what Caesar was? He was a piece of lint on the prophetic page of Scripture. That's all he was. Nothing more than a pawn in God's powerful hand. Remember what happened? A census was taken. A couple in Nazareth were forced to return to the place of their roots. So Joseph, being of the tribe of David, left for Bethlehem just in time. "When the fullness of time came," God moved in. And that's the way it is. That's the way it ALWAYS is.

Lacking the panorama of God's perspective, all we see are the outer limits of our one square. So we panic. "What will I do? How will I handle tomorrow? What about …? What if …? But …!" God says, "Trust Me. Just trust Me. Trust in Me with all your heart and don't lean on your own understanding. In all your ways acknowledge Me, and I'll direct your paths" (see Prov. 3:5–6).

What does Isaiah say? A frame of mind that is receiving support from leaning and is therefore being sustained, God will keep in "shalom, shalom." Because he casts everything on Him. Everything! And that includes unfulfilled dreams … unpleasant circumstances … and an uncertain future.

CONCLUSION

An Invitation

You may not know Jesus Christ personally. Your life may be filled with anxiety because of your business, your marriage, your children, your parents, your future, your money, your tomorrow. First things first. Peace begins with a Person. You can't legislate peace. We've learned that from the United Nations—what a study in futility! Peace is found in the person of Jesus Christ and I direct you to Him. Trust Him personally. Receive Him now. He died. He rose from the dead for you to give you His peace and to give you a whole new direction—that you might live peacefully with unfulfilled dreams and unpleasant circumstances and an uncertain tomorrow.

Cast yourself on the trampoline. Put all your weight on Him. He'll take you. Receive Him now.

Now Christian, what can be said to you? As an anxious individual you're not good company. You don't think clearly. You lose respect for yourself, and others ultimately lose it for you. If you're in a leadership position, you diminish your role. Ask God to give you a perspective of His whole moving gameboard, not just your own square. It will take away your panic, give you back your sleep and your sense of humor, and provide you with a new direction in life.

A Prayer

Our Father in heaven, through the increased pressure and the unexpected outcome of our lives, You have a way of reducing our lives to the irreducible minimum. We run out of crutches and it's at that point that You step in and say, "I've been here all the time. Remember, I am the permanent Rock."

Thank you for the timeless message that fell from the pen of Isaiah centuries ago . . . a message that still has a relevant ring to it today. I ask You to bring about a marvelous sense of relief, that release that comes only from leaning on You, Lord God. And bring those that never have met Your Son to a knowledge of Him. Show us again the truth of that gospel song we often sing but seldom model:

> What a fellowship, what a joy divine,
> Leaning on the everlasting arms;
> What a blessedness, what a peace is
>   mine,
> Leaning on the everlasting arms.
> Leaning, leaning,
> Safe and secure from all alarms;
> Leaning, leaning,
> Leaning on the everlasting arms.[2]

I pray in Jesus' Rock-like Name, Amen.

[1]*Quote/Unquote,* compiled by Lloyd Cory (Wheaton, Ill.: Victor Books, 1977), 232.

[2]Anthony J. Showalter, "Leaning on the Everlasting Arms," *Hymns for the Family of God* (Nashville, Tenn.: Paragon Associates, Inc., 1976), 87.

Other booklets by Chuck Swindoll:

Anger

Attitudes

Commitment

Dealing with Defiance

Demonism

Destiny

Divorce

Eternal Security

Fun is Contagious

God's Will

Hope

Impossibilities

Integrity

Leisure

The Lonely Whine of the Top Dog

Moral Purity

Our Mediator

The Power of a Promise

Prayer

Sensuality

Singleness

Stress

This is No Time for Wimps!

Tongues

When Your Comfort Zone Gets the Squeeze

Woman